ONE
RED
Rose

ONE RED Rose

ALMA REASOR

authorHOUSE®

AuthorHouse™
1663 Liberty Drive
Bloomington, IN 47403
www.authorhouse.com
Phone: 1-800-839-8640

Published by AuthorHouse   12/10/2014

ISBN: 978-1-4969-4880-9 (sc)
ISBN: 978-1-4969-4879-3 (e)

Any people depicted in stock imagery provided by Thinkstock are models,
and such images are being used for illustrative purposes only.
Certain stock imagery © Thinkstock.

This book is printed on acid-free paper.

Because of the dynamic nature of the Internet, any web addresses or links contained in this book may have changed
since publication and may no longer be valid. The views expressed in this work are solely those of the author and do
not necessarily reflect the views of the publisher, and the publisher hereby disclaims any responsibility for them.

KJV
Scripture quotations marked KJV are from the Holy Bible, King James Version (Authorized Version). First published
in 1611. Quoted from the KJV Classic Reference Bible, Copyright © 1983 by The Zondervan Corporation.

This is dedicated in beloved memory of my friend and sister in the Lord, Alma Reasor.

Alma sat down to rest

While Heaven was busy preparing for a special guest

Angels were summoned to usher her along for the journey is vast

But it's over in a flash

The plan was for Valentine's Day, but many of the saints were so anxious.

Especially, one they call Doc.

So God decided to set up the clock.

Alma thought she was alone, but she was surrounded by a heavenly throng.

When the Master calls there's no time for delay

But somehow Alma left us with a word to say

How she felt about her family and what summed up her life more appropriately

So she went above and left us with one word…Love!

Jack Tolbert

Contents

One Red Rose

Just one red rose
I give to thee
With all my love
To you from me

Just one red rose
I share with thee
And all our life
Share you with me, please?

CATEGORY

1

ANIMAL

A Little Ole' Flea and My Hound Dog

I'm just a tiny little ole flea
So tiny I'm very hard to see
Don't mean no trouble—just being me
I'm just a tiny little ole' flea
I jump up on that ole' hounds back
I have plenty energy to spare
I wiggle and giggle as I run to and fro
Through that ole' hounds hair
I jump up on his big ole' ear
Just to have a look inside
I find a hole that's plenty big
For a little ole' flea to hide
I like to dance and jump around
Kick, pinch, and have a bite
I like to dig my feet in good
So I can hold on tight
But that old hound
He don't share my fun
He just runs round and round
He howls and growls, snaps and bites
And finally flops on the ground
I'm just a tiny little ole' flea
So tiny I'm very hard to see
Don't mean no trouble—just being me
I'm just a tiny little ole' flea.

Close Acquaintance

The tiny grasshopper
Hops all day
Wishing there was someone
With whom he could play

The greasy fishing worm
Crawls through the ground
He has nothing to do
But wiggle around

The nasty old fly
With his dirty feet
Crawls over everything
We have to eat

The striped potato bug
Quiet as can be
Eats on our vegetables
Tho pretty is he

These close acquaintances
Are pests one by one
They pester the farmer
Till his work is done.

Friends

If I lay down
I'm long and slim
If I stand up
I'm tall and trim

I can run
Fast up a tree
Jump in a hole
And you can't find me

I can hoppy-hop
Through grass so thick
Dodge a hunter
Jump a creek

Friends of Nature
This we are
You will find us
Near and far

In memory
of Rowlen for his
grandchildren
Brock, Annah, Cadie & Trinety

Isn't It Great Just to Be Alive

Isn't it great just to be alive?
To breathe the good fresh air
To feel the sunshine on your face
To feel the wind blow your hair
Isn't it great just to be alive?

Isn't it great just to be alive?
To sit on the banks of a stream
To cool your feet in the water below
To feel the tug of a fish on your line
To watch the water softly flow
To hear a croak from the frog on the bank
To watch the glitter worm glow

Isn't it great just to be alive?
To see the flowers bloom in Spring
To see the fields green with grass
To hear the meadow lark sing
To see a squirrel crack a nut
To watch a wooly worm crawl
To see a dog chase a kitty cat
To hear a moo—cow bawl

Isn't it great just to be alive?
To breathe the good fresh air
To feel the sunshine on your face
To feel the wind blow your hair
Isn't it great just to be alive?

Victoria B.

Nature

Here I sit in the early morn
Watching the lift of the heavy fog
Listening to the crickets chirp their tune
Hearing the croak of the big green frog

Feeling the dew as it drips off the trees
Watching the squirrel run to and fro
Hearing the birds sing a melody of song
Looking at beautiful flowers as they continue to grow

Watching the sun as it creeps up o'er the hills
Seeing fish play around in the stream
Watching a chipmunk searching for food
Everything so quiet, peaceful, and serene

All these things of nature to enjoy
They are God's gift from up above
They were never earned by you and me
Just free gifts of God's great love

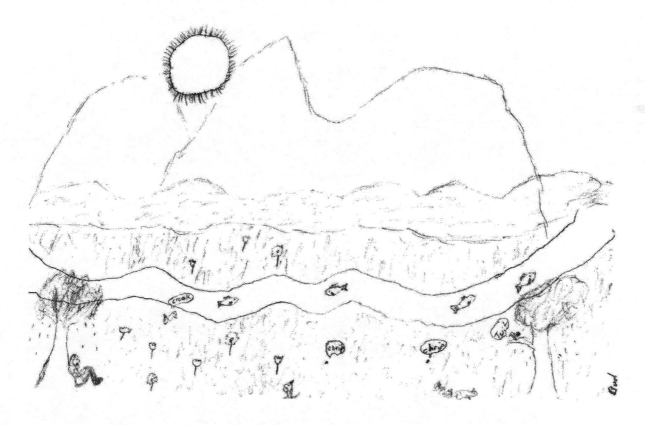

Nature Endures

A gravel road begins in the middle of nowhere
Winding up the side of a long steep hill
Old oak trees make a fence along each side
Surrounded by woods for miles around
Leaves have fallen in the autumn mist
While squirrels are jumping to and fro
Birds are singing their melody of song
As the wise old owl sits high in a tree
But—look—there—high upon a hill
The beauty soon fades away
The old two-story house with shutters torn
Window panes broken and roof caved in
Weatherboard split and paint all gone
Is slowly sliding down the side of the hill
Material things, of this world soon tumble and fall
These things we don't quite understand
But the beauty of nature will forever endure
For it was created by God's own hands

Peter Rabbit

Peter Rabbit with his cotton tail
Goes hippity hoppin down the bunny rabbit trail
He pauses here and he pauses there
And all the other animals just stand and stare
He stops to get him a bite to eat
Then on to see who he might meet
He says "Hello" to a friend or two
Well, it might be me or it might be you
He whistles as he goes his way
It helps him to pass the time of day
Peter Rabbit with his cotton tail
Goes hippity hoppin' down the bunny rabbit trail

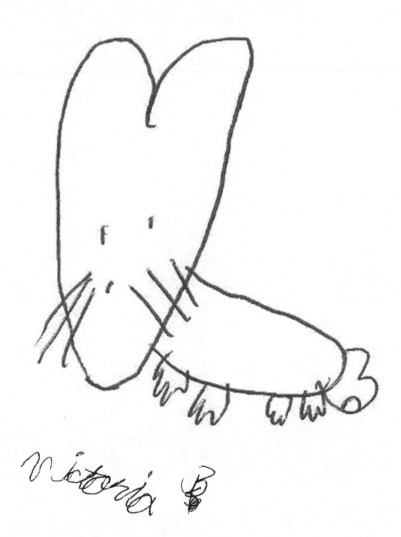

CATEGORY

2

CHILDREN

Alphabet

Say the alphabet
Start with A,B,C
Then continue on
With D,E,F,G
Now you're ready for H,I,J
Stop for a pause
Then K,L,M,N,O,P
Next must come Q,R,S,T
Last but not least
Are U,V,W,X,Y, and Z

Choo—Choo

I hear the choo—choo comin'
Its whistle's loud and clear
Hoooo-Hoooo-Hoooo
Chuggin' down the railroad track
For everyone to hear
Hoooo—Hoooo—Hoooo

I see the conductor smilin'
As the throttle he opens wide
I see the flagman wavin'
His arms from side to side
I see the black smoke rollin'
From the smokestack to the sky
I hear the children shoutin'
As the choo—choo chugs on by

I hear the choo—choo goin'
Its whistle's loud and clear
Hoooo—Hoooo—Hoooo
Chuggin' down the railroad track
For everyone to hear
Hoooo—Hoooo—Hoooo

Halloween

October is the month
The 31st is the day
We celebrate Halloween
In a very special way

The frost is on the pumpkin
The corn is in the shocks
As we go from house to house
And on the door we give a knock

And when the door is opened
We all hold out our hands
And yell "Trick or Treat"
They all seem to understand

For we're dressed up like witches and goblins
In weird suits and masks
And as spirits and scary ghosts
We give out sounds that last

Its lots and lots of fun
For the young and the old
As we sit in the dark and tell stories
That never seem to grow old

But we'll just sum it all up
Right now especially for you
In one little three letter word…..
BOO!

CATEGORY

3

DAD

Daddy

Daddy, Daddy none can compare
You're the greatest Daddy anywhere
A great big grin—a twinkle in your eye
You seldom pout and you never cry.

Daddy, Daddy you're so good to me
There will never be any as great as thee
I've looked and looked but none can I find
That's so gentle, so good, and so kind.

Daddy, Daddy you're all I could ask for
You carry the burdens—you conquer the task
You're a great Daddy, with patience galore
How could I ask for anything more?

Daddy, Daddy you're a Christian I know
You sow good seed wherever you go
Earth is just a place we're passing thru
But it's a much better place because of you.

Lonely Heart

It's lonely here in this heart of mine
But that's where I spend a lot of my time
Since you left and went so far away
It's so very hard to get through each day
I try to reach you; even call your name
But you never answer—Oh, I know you're not to blame
But if you could just answer and tell me what to do
I would be ever so grateful to you

I know that's not the way it was meant to be
I must get along without you, I can plainly see
So with God's help I will conquer the task
And hope that the time passes by very fast
Until we meet again in a much finer place
And meet our dear Savior face to face
But now—it's lonely here in this heart of mine
Since you left and went so far away
It's so very hard to get through each day

My Husband

How I used to sit and wait
To hear your footsteps on the walk
When from work you were returning
And I could hear you laugh and talk

How I miss your daily teasing
And little things you used to say
How I miss your good-night kisses
That you gave in a loving way

How I miss your arms about me
When I fall asleep at night
Oh! Just to hear you say you loved me
Then I'd know that all was right

You're the dearest, sweetest husband
That a woman could ever have
You are kind, you are loving
You are one who understands

Written in 1942 when I was homesick for
Jerry and he was in South Carolina.

To Jerry

He led me to you—a man
With great courage, strong will
Wisdom and understanding
Who has loved me, cherished me
And took care of me
Who has been a great Daddy
To all of our children
Who has worked hard for us
Giving us all the material things we need—and more
He who has guided us
And strengthened us in our faith in God
Stands beside all of us in times of trouble
Even tho sometimes we're in the wrong
Helps all his fellow man
Whenever he can
So I give to you all I have to give
Just three little words…
"All my love"

Alma

CATEGORY

4

DEATH

Silly Teen-agers

They laughed they giggled sometimes even cried
But usually they just looked deep into each other's eyes
As they run through the clover field hand in hand
A couple silly teen-agers, folks didn't understand.

The love that they carried deep in their hearts
Was something no one could ever tear apart
The days slipped by as they made their plans
A couple silly teen-agers, folks didn't understand.

Way out in the country, high upon a hill
The little white church-house stands there still
Where they took their vows sealed with a kiss
A couple silly ten-agers, folks were gonna miss.

They packed their clothes and jumped into a car
Their destination was really not very far
Jobs in the country could hardly be found
So a couple silly teen-agers, were moving to town.

But they never reached the city that day
Because a terrible crash occurred on the way
In the front seat of the car, still holding hands
Died two silly teen-agers folks didn't understand.

Someday

One of these days
It will all be over
One of these days
It will all be past
There'll be no heartache
There'll be no sorrow
There'll be no pain
And no tomorrows
One of these days
It will all be over
One of these days
It will all be past
We'll be with Jesus
Just wait and see
We'll live with him
Through Eternity

Lent For Awhile

"I'll lend you for a little while,
A child of mine", he said
For you to love the while she lives,
And mourn for, when she's dead.
It may be six or seven years,
Or twenty—two or three,
But will you, till I call her back,
Take good care of her for me?

She'll bring her charms to gladden you,
And should her stay be brief,
You'll have her lovely memories
As solace for your grief
I cannot promise she will stay
Since all from earth return,
But there are lessons taught down there
I wish this child to learn.

I've looked the wide world over
In my search for teachers true,
And from the throngs that crowd life's lanes,
I have selected you.
So you must give her all your love,
Do not think the labour vain
And don't hate me when I come
To call to take her back again.

I fancied that I heard them say,
Dear Lord, thy will be done.
For all the joy thy child shall bring.
The risk of grief I'll run.
We'll shelter her with tenderness,
We'll love her while we may,
And for the happiness we've known,
Forever grateful stay.

And should the angels call for her,
Much sooner than we've planned,
We'll brave then bitter grief that comes
And try so hard to understand.

Written in memory of Kresta Jane Wineinger

CATEGORY

5

FAMILY

Cold Picture

Two rosy cheeks that smart with cold
Stars sparkle and dance in her shiny blue eyes
Soft red lips that are turning pale blue
And a pink shiny nose pointed up to the skies
As I look out through my dark window pane
A beautiful framed face I can see
Cause there through the fluffy white snow flakes
Is my own darling daughter, looking back at me. (Kay)

Looking out my kitchen window while cooking supper.

Grandmother

I remember in days gone by,
Dear Grandmother she would say
"Alma, before you get in bed
Don't forget to pray."

Grandmother always was religious,
The Bible was before her all the time,
And never did a day go by,
But what she read a line.

She would tell us little stories,
As we gathered round her bed,
And then when she was finished,
She'd say, "Now bow your head."

"Dear God who art in heaven
We pray to Thee tonight
That I may help these children
See the good old Gospel light."

I can still see dear old Grandmother
Leaving this old world of sin
She was going up to Heaven,
For God to receive her in.

I can see her up in Heaven
With the angels gathered round
And I know that they were with her,
When we laid her in the ground.

Inward Confusion.....Outward Silence

I bet you didn't even notice today
When all the family was gathered round
With all of you talking, joking, and laughing
That I seldom ever made a sound.

All of you were talking about something special
I listened carefully, but couldn't quite hear
So I asked Who? What? When? Where?
But no one had time to lend an ear.

Some of you grinned; looked at each other
Shrugged your shoulders in disgust and dismay
So I closed my mouth, put a grin on my face
And thought surely there would be a better day.

I guess some of the questions I ask you
Or things I talk about from time to time
Does seem quite silly to young folk like you
But its things that seem to clutter my mind.

I know this is all a part of growing old
As my face is clouded with dreadful fears.
But please take time—try a little to understand
As down my face escapes a few wet tears.

Mamma And Her Little Girl

I am your mamma, I nursed you
Then I saw you weaned
I saw you as you learned to crawl
In diapers white and clean
I saw you waddle to and fro
As you began to walk
I heard you stutter and sputter
As you began to talk
I saw your soft golden hair
Lay in curls around your face
I saw you dressed in red, cushy, velvet
And white frilly, fancy lace
I saw your rosy cheeks
Blue eyes shining bright
Your ruby red lips in a smile
That said, "Everything's alright."
I saw your soft golden hair
Turn to a mousy brown
You soon became the envy
Of every girl in town
I saw the way the boys
All grinned and sighed at you
It was the way they winked
As they said, "How do you do?"
You were my little girl
But too soon to a lady grew
I hardly had enough time
To get well acquainted with you
And now our days of family life
Are about to come to an end
Because you see my teen-age girl
Has found her a new friend
So here you are my little girl
You just marched down the aisle
In a beautiful, long, white wedding gown
And wearing a great big smile
Walking down that road of life
Where our family life comes to an end
And finding at the end of the rainbow
That tall, handsome, wonderful friend
As your hands touched and your lips met
Here at the rainbows end
May God tie a knot that will never break
Between my little girl and her friend.

Memories Of Days Gone By

Today was a day that we didn't need food
To give us life or keep us in a good mood
We have lived on memories of days gone by
Sometimes we've laughed, sometimes cried
We remember too well the day you were born
Two tiny little girls who looked so forlorn
Your face was so red, your skin all wrinkled
But when you opened your eyes oh! How they twinkled
You drank your milk, wet your pants sometimes
You cooed, you giggled, smiled from time to time
Soon you sat up, then crawled, then began to talk
First thing you knew you had entered school
Then you began to think you were really cool
You could laugh, play or sometimes even plot
But when it came to work you sometimes forgot
Learning while growing was important to you
But bowling and parties were also things to do
You two are the last of a family of eight
Now you're gone out on your own to meet your own fate
Now Daddy and I are back where we began
Sharing, laughing, planning having fun
So maybe each of you will drop in sometimes
Or if too far away—then drop us a line
So you see there'll never be a day that we need food
To give us life or keep us in a good mood
We'll just live on memories of days gone by
Sometimes we'll laugh, sometimes we'll cry.

My Brother

I have a brother
Who is very special to me
Just the two of us left
Out of our family

So what can I give him
What can I do
That would be very special
For just us two

He doesn't need money
Or anything it can buy
And God sent him His blessings
Down from the sky

So I will just give him
A very special part
Of all of the love for him
I have in my heart

And let him know
He's very special to me
'Cause we're all that's left
Of our family

My Little Girl
"Lynn"

With a shake of my hand, I said good-bye
Tears were beginning to fill my eyes
I kissed your cheek and hurried out the door
It was time to part again, once more,
As I went to leave, with a wave of my hand,
I tried to say "Darling, I understand."
But wherever I go or whatever I do,
I shall never erase that picture of you,
For there you stood in the frame of the door
Hair hanging down, your head bent o'er,
Tears streaming down your pretty face,
Trying to be brave, trying not to weep.
Even tho now with a home of your own
You carry with you the memories of home.
Can't you see Darling—Can't you see?
It isn't easy for you and it's hard for me
But this is the way it was meant to be,
God laid the plans for you and for me
We'll accept this plan like all the rest
Because we know that God knows best.

Nancy

You are a darling daughter,
A true gift in every way,
You are just the kind of daughter,
I asked God to send one day.

You're a very lovely woman,
Your face with happiness glows,
Your smile—the twinkle in your eyes
Your heart must be made of pure gold.

You're a special, wonderful wife,
No man could ask for anything more
You're true, kind, thoughtful and good,
You give out of your love galore.

But most of all you're the grandest Mother,
A child's dream come true
The love you give to your children,
Could only come from a Mother like you!

Your Mamma

Written to Nancy Walters on Mother's Day 1972

Noni

A chubby little blue-eyed girl
With light brown hair that laid in curls
With rosy cheeks and lips so red
An angel from heaven I often said
A big cheery smile, a twinkle in your eye
Seldom a pout, a whimper, or a cry
Joy, laughter, and love all day through
Who could help but love a little girl like you
Knowledge in your noggin, wisdom in your hands
Music in your heart from far off lands
Now your hair has turned to a mousy brown
You were the envy of every boy in town
They were shy-you were shy
So you both just looked and sighed
Your days were noisy, your nights were fun
You were always on the run
Busy, busy as any mother bee
I guess that was how it was meant to be
The honor roll-one-two-three-four
I know you could have made it more
National Honor Society put your name on its scroll
The Tri-Hi-Y added your name to its roll
The Short Hand award you accepted with pride
The medals you won you took in stride
Tonight, I watched you march down the aisle
I saw a tear, a quiver, then a smile
You graduated tonight with honors galore
You couldn't dream of asking for more
As the music played I watched some more
I saw you turn and march out the door
I thought to myself as you faded from view
That chubby little girl to a woman grew
With your rosy cheeks and lips so red
There goes my angel I softly said.

Our Indiana Home

We just received a letter from home
The place that will always seem so near
Mother sent us all her tender love
And we received a kiss from Daddy Dear

The boys they both wished us lots of luck
And sister wished us happiness galore
Auntie said she wished us lots of fun
Grandpa hopes that we'll be happy evermore

It's wonderful to hear the news from home
And to paint a picture in our minds
Of the children round the little cottage door
Of the Indiana home we left behind

Just to see the roses blooming in the spring
As they go winding up the wall
To see the birds come flying back again
And hear the whipper-will begin his call

The children picking berries in the sun
As they have to do on summer days
To see them swimming in the pond
When work is o'er and time for play

These are just a few of my memories
That suddenly come flashing through my mind
As we are now so very far away
From the Indiana home we left behind

Written in 1943 when we were in South Carolina

Precious Memories

We got a houseful of youngens
Tis a sight to behold
And we'll never have money
Nor silver-nor gold
But we'll have precious memories
As the years they unfold
To discuss by the fireside
As we're growing old.

Rowlen

It seems like only yesterday
That you were a chubby little lad
With big blue eyes open wide
That sometimes looked so sad
Mousy brown hair that flopped
Around on your old top knot
Sometimes it was hard to tell it
From the old kitchen mop
Sweet pink lips that quivered
When everything wasn't right
But could give the sweetest kisses
When you went to bed at night
How you could howl with a finger hurt
And come crying to the door
"Kiss it mamma kiss it
Now, kiss it some more."
Then we had a little boy
Full of all kinds of jokes and fun
Healthy, happy all day long
Able to play, jump, and run
But soon you grew to a teenage son
Your childish days were o'er
That girl had taken mamma's place
You had time to play no more
Daddy and I have had our dreams
We watched you grow each day
We hope that we have been a help
In showing you the way
Now graduation day is here
Our son will soon be a man
I'm sure our dreams, your dreams
Will come true-I know they can
'Cause you have what it takes my son
You've proven that before
To be whatever you want to be
You can be rich or poor
I know that you will surely do
The very best you can
And you will be great for those who care—
Mom and Dad, and for God, and Man.

That Little Old House By The Roadside

That little old house by the roadside
That's over a hundred years old
With vines growing up the wall
It's still as good as gold

But the poor family that lives there
Just don't get any rest
Because every Sunday and weekdays too
There comes those awful pests

Company, company that's all we see
Some folks stay all week
And are we glad when they're all gone
Cause then we can get some sleep

Laying all those jokes aside
We're glad when you all come
And hope that all the time you're here
That you have lots of fun

Written on a Sunday afternoon in 1938 when Harley and Dorothy
Hanaver were at our house. This was the first poem I wrote.

That Little White Cottage

Remember that little white cottage that you promised me?
You kept saying—later maybe some other time
Well the days passed into weeks, weeks
into months, months into years
And the years just passed into time
Our family came to us rather quickly
A girl first—then two boys so fair
A girl was number four-then five, also six
The last two girls just came in a pair
We were so busy just trying to raise them
And having them something to eat
Helping bathe them—making their clothes
And keeping shoes on their feet
Trying to tell them how much God and us loved them
Teaching them they were ever so unique
Showing them how to love and get along with each other
And how all of this would make their life complete
By now I vaguely remember-
That little white cottage that you promised me
And how you said—later maybe some other time
Well time has passed swiftly, no time left to ponder
You now have a home of a much better kind, so I'll just dream on
Of that little white cottage that you promised me
And I'll say—later all in due time
For the years will pass swiftly and Jesus will soon call me
And I'll have that little white cottage, no doubt in my mind

Two Little Angels

God had two little angels
And He looked everywhere
For just the right parents
Who would love them with care

Then He sent them to earth
With a mission in mind
And He said, "If you'll seek
Someday you'll find"

They were so cuddly and warm
They just wiggled and squirmed
They grinned and they gooed
And their grip was quite firm

We fed them when hungry
And rocked them at night
We bathed them and changed them
And done things just right

They were chubby little girls
And soon began to crawl
First one step then two steps
It seemed like no time at all

Then off they went to kindergarten
One beautiful fall
Our two little angels
Were growing quite tall

Then next year to grammar school
Together—they went
And eight wonderful years
In this school they spent

Then on to high school
And all of the while
They fussed—they argued
But they always wore a smile

They were happy and lucky
Seldom ever did they cry
Our angels were growing up
And the years were passing by
But we were just as happy
As earthly mortals could be
Just papa and mamma
Little Bo and Dee

Then one day quite suddenly
We all realized
The mission God had sent them on
Was before our very eyes

For you see:
They were sent to aging parents
To share their love, their joy, their laughter
So now their mission they have found
We'll go on living happy ever after.

CATEGORY

6

FRIENDSHIP

A Special You!

You just remember
And don't you ever forget
We all love you a bunch
So get well quick
We're waiting, we're anxious
For your return
We're hoping, we're praying
We're very concerned
Work with them earnestly
Make no mistake
You're gutsy, you're sturdy
You've got what it takes
Keep that pretty smile
And that twinkle in your eyes
Hold on to your faith
And hold your chin up high
With God there beside you
To lead the way
Good doctors and nurses
What more can I say
Except------
You just remember
And don't you ever forget
We all love you a bunch
So get well quick!

Love Between Friends

The love between two friends
Is a very special love
It is not woven lightly
And when it's woven
It can never be raveled
Because the weave is woven tightly.

CATEGORY

7

LOVE

Another Place—Another Time

The happiness we shared
As time turned into years
Came to a sudden end
And laughter turned to tears
You had to go away
And leave me behind
We can't build a bridge
Between your place and mine
Our love that we once knew
Our love that was sublime
No one else can have
It's yours and it's mine
So we will just pretend
That everything is fine
Until we meet again
Another place—another time

Written in 1991

59

Better Life

We smiled at each other, hugged each other, kissed each other, loved
  each other
That's how life began for us in our younger years
We talked together, made plans together, dreamed together, had visions
  together
Never having any doubts or fears
We had our good times, bad times, happy times, sad times
Just like most humans you see
We laughed together, cried together, played together, worked together
We thought that was how life was meant to be
We went to church together, sang together, prayed together and
  worshiped together
We knew God wanted it that way
We raised our family together, loved them together, taught them
  together, spanked them together
They grew up and moved away
Then God smiled on you, took your hand and led you
Now you are no longer near
Tho God's always beside me, holds my hand and guides me
There's loneliness and many a tear
With family all around me and their love surrounds me
There's a hollow place that just won't go away—I need loving arms
  around me
A firm voice to assure me
That life will get better as time passes away
These things that I long for, hope for, and pray for
I'm assured they will be coming my way
So I won't have to weep—can close my eyes and go to sleep
And know that life will be better at breaking of day

Don't You Love Me Anymore Little Darling?

Don't you love me anymore little darling?
Don't you care when I'm sad and when I'm blue?
Don't you care when the days seem dark and lonely?
Don't you care when I cry for only you?

Don't you love me anymore little darling?
Don't you care because they've called me away?
Don't you care because my life is in danger?
Fighting for you day after day?

Don't you love me anymore little darling?
Don't you care when I say I dream of you?
When I gave up all I owned for the Army
Just to fight for the ol' red, white, and blue?

Oh! I'll always love you little darling.
And I hope your answer to this will be yes,
So that when this terrible war is over,
I'll come back and we'll find our happiness.

Written in 1942 for a soldier to send home to the girl he loved.

Happy Birthday

Neither of us spoke a single word
But as we turned and our eyes met
We both knew right from that moment
That neither of us would e'er forget

We held hands when we went walking
Kissed as we passed each other by
Put loving arms around each other
Vowed our love until we died

Life's been very good to both of us
Along the way we've shared good health
We've had good times—sometimes bad
We've seen poverty—also wealth

Tis so good these years together
Our love we still share day after day
We laugh, we cry, we sometimes joke
We wouldn't want it any other way

We know today our love grows stronger
As the years swiftly pass us by
Today you have another birthday
And I don't know if I should laugh or cry!

Victoria B.

He

He can place his arm around my shoulder
Pat my hand and sooth away my fears
Let me lay my head on his arm to sleep
And when I cry, wipe away my tears.

He can brush a lock of hair from my forehead
Wink at me where no one else can see
Place his lips softly upon mine
That's why he's so special to me.

How I Love You

Oh how I love you
Words cannot say
Their sound—their meaning
There's just no way

Oh how I love you
I cannot express
In all my emotions
In all my distress

Oh how I love you
My feelings must show
As the years slip by
And my love grows

Look at me—look at me
Look deep in my eyes
Can't you see that I love you
And will till I die?

I Wonder?

Years have come and years have gone
Since the first time I met you
And I wonder tonight Dear
If you still feel the way I do?

Thunder rolled all round about us
Grey clouds have their shadows dealt
Lightening flashed so close it shook us
Many storms their weather we felt

Falling tears the rain clouds shed
Heavy snows a blanket made
Twinkling stars have sparked o'er us
Sunshine laid us in its shade

We've had our share of joy and laughter
Peace, contentment were in our lot
Happiness, good health we've had together
Our share of earthly wealth we've got

Earth has dealt us many sorrows
Dark despair—we cannot explain
Sickness—even lost some loved ones
Yet through all of this my love remains

Years have come and years have gone
Since the first time I met you
And I wonder tonight, Dear
If you still feel the way I do?

Jerry

There's one boy that comes to our house
Who is no relation you see
He never mentions love
Nor his kind little wife to be
So sometimes I just wonder
What he comes to our house for
He never comes into the house
But sits out in the car.

My mommy says to me one day
You know what them fellers are
That goes to see a nice little girl
And sits out in the car.
You better watch 'em they're no good
Always makin' trouble you see
And my mommy says if I don't watch
He'll make plenty trouble for me.

I just told my mommy
I didn't believe a word she said
And if she'd see my Jerry
It sure would change her head.
Cause he's tall—not too handsome
His hair is almost blond
He's got the prettiest big blue eyes
You ever looked upon.

He's just a big old country hick
Who really never dresses very fine
He don't care how he combs his hair
Or whether or not he's on time
He's so silly—not dignified
Like the boys you see in town
And I'm tellin' you he's more fun
(When a great big crowd's around.)

And deep down in my silly heart
I guess my mommy's right
About them boys that sits in the car
And won't come in where it's light
But I wouldn't let my mommy know
How he acts in the dark
'Cause if I did, my mommy
Wouldn't even let me spark.

Written in 1941 while I was going with Jerry,
awhile before he left for the Army

66

Just You and Me

We were meant for each other
That we both can plainly see
We've been so happy together
Happiness was just meant to be.

Remember the night you said you loved me
And you'd never break my heart
That promise you have surely kept dear
Though we're many miles apart.

All the good times we had together
All the love words that we'd say
They are gone but not forgotten
They're within my heart to stay.

You'll never know how much I miss you
I think of you both night and day
You'll never know how much I pray dear
For you while you're gone away.

Uncle Sam won't keep you forever
Someday you'll be back
And just remember your sweethearts waiting
In that little old country shack.

Written in 1942 to Gerald while he was in service.

Last Love

Put your arms around me and hold me tenderly
Whisper all those words that seem to rhyme
Tell me all the things you meant to tell me all these years,
But somehow never seemed to find the time
Kiss my lips softly as you wipe away each tear
Brush away the lock of hair that down my forehead creeps
Look into my eyes and say you love me one more time
As I close my eyes in death and fall asleep.

Love

A friendly love is the love of a man
Who chats with the young and the old
Who laughs when they laugh cries when they cry
And their burdens just seem to unfold

A protective love is the love of a mother
As she fondles her first new born
Nature has provided food for hunger
And she wraps it up snugly to keep it warm

Just puppy love between a boy and a girl
But a love that's not easily broken
Just a look, a sigh, a clasp of the hands
And very few words softly spoken

The bond of love between a husband and a wife
Is a love that overflows from their heart
For better for worse were their wedding vows
And only death could tear them apart

But the greatest love that ever existed
Is the love Christ has for you and me
He shed His blood on the old rugged cross
Redeemed our sins and set us free

Love Me—Tell Me So

You see I'm just not able
To do all the things you do
I don't have the strength and energy
To run around with you
You go out in town at night
And I sit here all alone
Just watching television
Or talking on the phone
Then you come in and glance at me
And I know you really try
To hide the sadness and the tears
That shows within your eyes
I'm sure God has his reason
For making life this way
And I know I'm not to question why
But go on day after day
You know I will always love you
For you are just a part
Of all the dreams and wishes
That are hidden in my heart
So won't you take a little time
To dry away my tears
Put your arms around me
And soothe away my fears
Whisper words of comfort
Never, ever let me go but
Please don't look at me with pity
Just love and tell me so.

Marriage

Marriage is a bond that's sealed
Between two people who are in love
It's a gift not earned but given
From our Master from above.

You Once Said You Loved Me

Oh! Darling you once said you loved me
But all you said you done forgot
You turned my heart and then you broke it
And threw away the key and lock

When first we met was in Indiana
When the strawberries were in bloom
You said, "Darling please write me a letter
And I'll answer it real soon."

But when strawberry time was over
You turned and went your homeward way
I looked and looked for just one letter
I hoped you'd answer mine someday

But you never did answer my letter
Still I waited at the gate
I thought that someday you would answer
But Darling someday it'll be too late

Strawberry time is here again
Today is the thirtieth day of May
And still I pray to God in heaven
You'll return to me someday

Written May 30, 1940 to John Edward Goldman.

CATEGORY

8

HAPPY

Dreams

What would it be like if we didn't dream dreams
Of a cabin, a mansion, or a little teepee
Or a tiny white cottage down on the lake
Or whatever our desires might be?

What would it be like if we didn't dream dreams
Of a husband, a wife, and a home?
The pitty-patter of wee tiny feet
Just a family to claim as our own.

What would it be like if we didn't dream dreams
Or set for ourselves a goal
Or work or strive at meeting the task
Of satisfying the soul?

What would it be like if we didn't dream dreams
Of walking on the Kings Highway
Hand in hand with the Lord Jesus Christ
On that great Resurrection Day?

What would it be like if we didn't dream dreams
I really don't want to know!

Rain

Rain, rain, go away
Come again some other day
I'm on vacation, wanta stay
Wanta run, jump, and play
Wanta ride, see the sights
Wanta go out every night
Wanta swim, swim some more
Pick up sea shells on the shore
On the hot sand let me lay
Build up castles all the day
Build those castles, build them high
On the sand or in the sky
Wanta loaf--just be lazy
But now my dreams are getting hazy
You have ruined them all it seems
You have scattered all my dreams
Rain, rain go away
Come again some other day.

Sandman

The sandman's peepin' round your windowsill
Hush, little baby now please be still
He's gonna sprinkle sand in your eyes
Hush little baby now please don't cry
Close your little eyes and go to sleepy town
Sleep so very, very sound
Dream sweet dreams far into the night
Till you wake with morn's twilight.

Santa Claus

In a bright red suit, all trimmed in white
A tassel on his cap, that looked just right
A wide black belt, held his pants in place
He wore big black boots, with long black laces
A great big smile as he said, "Hello"
A tummy that jiggled like a bowl of Jell-O
The stars in his eyes just twinkled and shined
And the love in his heart was warm and kind
On his back was a pack heaped high with toys
He brought for the good little girls and boys
He'd had lots of help from his little elves
But a lot of the work he had done himself
The reindeer guided his sled with ease
As they made their rounds on Christmas Eve
Who is this man? What's his name?
Is he for real or is he playing a game?
If you are a person who really believes
In spirits and fairies on Christmas Eve
Then he's for real and he's not playing a game
And old Santa Claus is this man's name.

Sleep My Baby

Sleep my baby sleep
While Mother watches you
Dream sweet dreams of yore
All the long night through
Close your little ole eyes
That sparkle with delight
Sleep my baby sleep
Sleep till morn's twilight

Reasor Hope

CATEGORY

9

MOTHER

A Mother's Prayer

Oh! Lord as I come before Thee
Humbly I ask, as only a mother can
With all my heart,
That you might grant unto me the knowledge
To be able to understand thy word,
The wisdom to do thy will
The courage to stand up for right in all things
Good health and strength to be able to work for Thee
And help me, Lord, always to seek for truth and righteousness
Then, Lord, grant me the privilege
Of passing these things on to our children,
That you have so kindly loaned to us
For a short time here on earth
That we might all as a family be able to say,
"I not only believe in God, I know God."
When our mission on earth is over
Grant oh Lord, that not one soul
Of this precious family might be lost
But that we might all live forevermore in heaven,
With Thee throughout eternity.

In Jesus name,

Amen

A Special Mother's Day

I could go down to the variety store
With a nickel or a dime
And get a big and beautiful card
With a long and flowery rhyme
It would look so good
As you could plainly see
And you'd be so pleased
Cause it came from me
But that's not what I'd like to do
Nor what I had in mind
As we mark another Mother's Day
On the calendar of time
I'd like to open up my heart
And let you see what's there
The joy, the love, the happiness
For all of us to share
And the only reason, I have all of this
Is because of you this day
That's why Mother's Day is a very special day
In a very, very special way.

Do You Think He Knew?

What a privilege—what an honor
To have been chosen—with just a few
A Christian Mother—to bear God's children
Do you think He really knew?
Do you think Jesus really knew?
Knew all the secrets of my heart
Knew just what kind of mother
I would be—right from the start
Did He know I would love His children
He has so kindly loaned to me?
Did He hear the prayers I prayed
Night-after-night upon my knees?
Did He know I would lead their footsteps
In the path He would have them trod
Teach them to love their fellow man
Teach them about Jesus and almighty God?
Help me Jesus—please—help me
This is my prayerful plea
Help me mold their newborn souls
Into better souls for Thee
Oh what a privilege—what an honor
To have been chosen—with just a few
A Christian Mother—to bear God's children
Yes—I'm sure He always knew.

Mother

Nag, nag, nag, that's all I remember
Of the words and voice of one called Mother.

Put on your shoes, tie the lace,
Wash behind your ears, wipe off your face,
Pick up your papers, stack your books
Don't play with frogs, don't fall in the brook
Don't play in the rain, you'll get all wet
Don't fight, cry, scrap, or fret
Put away your toys, clean up your mess
Put on a smile, always look your best
Pick up your towel, hang it on the rack
Clean under your nails, scrub your back
Wear your toboggan, wrap up tight
Polish your shoes so they shine just right
Don't wear eye shadow, it will ruin your sight
Wipe off that lipstick it's much too bright
Turn the radio down, play the tape very soft
The television, you may just turn off
Read your bible, on Sundays go to church
Share love with your family and do your work
Don't gamble your money or drink a lot
Don't drive fast cars or stay out late
Always be true to your children and mate
Share Jesus with others who seem to be lost
Guide their footsteps to the foot of the cross.

Yes, her dear voice I well remember
I am what I am because of love from Mother.

My Mother

I recall glad memories
Of when I sat on Mother's knee
Stories of our dear Savior
She would kindly tell to me
She would sing a little chorus
She would help me say my prayers
She would kiss me on the cheek
Then a stroke upon my hair
She was often very busy
When a favor would I ask
But she took time out to help me
From her burden and her task
If I got hurt or was in trouble
Somehow she was always there
Just to comfort and console me
With kind words and loving care
She has brought me up with Jesus
She has taught me how to pray
As I journey along life's pathway
As I walk and talk each day
Nothing else can ever help me
Like my Mother's shining face
There's just no one like my Mother
There's no one can take her place
I thank the Lord for my dear Mother
And I'm glad that she's not gone
And is here in times of trouble
Just to guide me right from wrong

Written in 1950 for my Mom.

Searched

I heard a preacher preach today
"It's Mother's Day" he proudly said
With words, a picture of Mother he painted
Like the one I'd so often read
Mother is one of the sweetest people
God ever put on earth
Her kiss can heal a bump
Till it doesn't even hurt.
She's gentle, ever so gentle
Handles everyone with loving care
Soothes a brow all dripping with sweat
Takes away all worries and fear
She has patience like you wouldn't believe
Can calm the toughest mob
Wipe away a tear, read a poem
And quiet the loudest sob
She's ever so kind to any and all
Like Jesus would want her to be
She could feed a thief if he was hungry
She has never met a stranger you see
I listened to that preacher a half hour or more
The picture of Mother I could plainly see
I listened, I looked, I tried so hard to find
But I never did recognize me!

CATEGORY

10

PATRIOTIC

Our Nation's Heroes

The planes swarmed in the sky that day
They dropped those bombs like flies
On the innocent people of America
Of whom many lost their lives

Uncle Sam has called the girl's young sweethearts
He has called our Mother's sons
He has called the wives' dear husbands
To the battle front as one

We're proud to say we're Americans
And we all can stand the strife
Until our men are free to come home again
And we can have our dreams of life

But it's useless to hope this war over
We'll not stop until we've won
And that will be sometime yet
As Uncle Sam has just begun

Take Washington at Valley Forge
Cold weather—nothing to eat
We're proud to say that battle
Came out without defeat

And John Paul Jones when his own vessel
Was shot from beneath his feet
He sailed away in a captured one
Not taken from the U.S. Fleet

Now these are just examples
Of what the old U.S. has done
We never leave a battle
Until it's thoroughly won

We still have the blood of our forefathers
Running warmly in our veins
We'll send those slant-eyed Japanese
Back from where they came

Then our heroes will come back
To the land they have fought to own
And find their sweethearts, wives, and Mothers
Waiting for them back home

Written for Jerry in 1942

CATEGORY

11

RELIGIOUS

Age—Death

Age—I am so afraid of you…..
Afraid of the unknown and what you will do
Afraid of the things I cannot see
Afraid of all the changes you will make in me

Death—I am so afraid of you…..
Afraid of the unknown and what you will do
Afraid of the things I cannot see
Afraid of the changes you will make in me

So age do I have a choice to grow old with you
And stay on earth these years tho they be few
Or die in death and meet all my fears
I have secretly harbored all these years

The choice is not mine to make
God alone gives—God alone takes
So with God's help I will struggle through
And meet you both head on—my task I'll do

When age goes and death comes, God will take my hand
And lead me home to the Promised Land
So age—death go hide your face
I will conquer my fears in this ole' place

Then I'll make that journey to Heaven's gate
I don't want to be early—don't want to be late
But with my hand in His and with His love and grace
I will meet my dear Savior FACE TO FACE

A Dream

Late last night as I lay in my bed
My eyelids began to flutter in sleep
I began to dream—I think it was a dream
And then I drifted off to sleep

I was going on a trip, a very long trip
The road was wide and crooked as could be
There were a lot of people just wandering around
And I couldn't see what lay ahead of me
But I didn't mind, twas a jolly good crowd
Everyone was happy, so gay and so free
It was mostly friends who I already knew
And they were so glad to see me
We laughed and joked as we went along
We had traveled together before
Eventually we'd reach the end of the road
And then we'd meet many, many more
Far off in the distance a faint laughter we heard
It soon developed into a mighty roar
There sat the Devil, like a king on his throne
Gathering his sheep to the share
Too late we realized the road we had taken
And our laughter turned into a moan
There was weeping, begging, and gnashing of teeth
And our prayers turned into groans

Late last night as I lay in my bed
My eyelids began to flutter in sleep
I began to dream—I know now it was a dream
For I awoke and began to weep

A Family Pew

I went back home tonight to the little country church
They were celebrating old fashion day, they said
The men were dressed in overalls, the women wore long dresses
And God's word, the Bible, they softly read

As I sit in my pew my mind wondered back
To the days of yesteryear and I could almost feel
My family setting right there by my side
Oh! It all seemed so sweet and so real

As the old fashion gospel hymns were sung
Daddy sang tenor, mamma alto, I just sang naturally
My brothers didn't sing very much at all
But we worshiped together as a Christian family

Daddy was an elder in the little country church
He led the sheep—help set them apart
His prayers weren't flowery no big fancy words
Just words of love he spoke from his heart

Mamma taught Sunday School from the days of her youth
She taught nothing but the true word of God
She taught many a youngster, the youth and the old folks
And set their feet on the path they should trod

My mind was jolted back to the time and the place
It had only been a dream or a kind of fantasy
But maybe someday I'll share a pew again
In Heaven with Christ and my Christian family

A Talk with Jesus

I'm sure you've noticed lately, Jesus
Just how lazy I have been
I haven't sung a song for you
Or read a poem—but then
You know I've had those terrible headaches
My stomach hurts, my eyes are blurred
I don't think straight or talk too good
For you see my speech is slurred
Now that's just about all the excuses
I can come up with right now
So looks like I better just get to work
And do my part…..somehow
I'm not really very smart
I need to learn…..not teach
I can sing a little—but not professionally
And I'm sure I could never preach
I can't do heavy labor work
Like clean the church or mow the lawn
Because you see I'm getting older
I don't have strength in my hands and arms
But I'm sure there must be something
Tho it be little—that I can do
Some kind of work—today—Jesus
I can do—just especially for you
So with your help—Jesus—I can write a poem
And read it for others, as well as me
So that as Christians—together we
Might all enjoy and let the whole world see
Just how much we love our Jesus
And want to work for you each day
For we really do love you Jesus
Even tho sometimes we find excuses, get lazy
And go astray

A Talk with the Lord

Here I lay, in my bed, fully awake
Eyes open wide, staring at the ceiling
I really can't see, for it's dark, it's night
And I have such a weird, funny, feeling.

So I'll talk with you for a while, tonight, Lord
Although I'm sure you already know
The things I want to talk about Lord
Are the things that worry me so.

I've taught her right from wrong, Lord
And she knows all about you
She's a good girl, Lord you know
And she knows what you want her to do.

I don't really worry about her being good
For I know she's in your hands
But sometimes the things she continues to do
Lord, I just can't quite understand.

My mind wanders back through the years, Lord
And many memories I call to mind
Some of them heartache and trouble
But some of them are pleasant and kind.

I've kissed her bruises—one by one
I've wiped away many a tear
I've held her hand when she was sick
I've soothed away many a fear.

I watched her go, her first day at school
Her new dress she so proudly portrayed
I saw her in her first recital
When the piano she so softly played.

I saw her accept her awards with pride
As she timidly marched down the aisle
I saw her on graduation night
As she wore a great big smile.

I've talked to her, Lord, many a time
When things didn't go just right
And when she was troubled or worried, Lord
I've prayed for her most all night.

The little light in the window, Lord
Is still burning and its break of dawn
Her footsteps will be heavy,
Her eyelids droopy, her mouth in a yawn

But I guess she don't understand, Lord
'Cause you know it's only a mother's love
That's why I'm laying awake now, Lord
Asking you for help from above.

A Visit

I open one eye—then the other
Reluctantly I turn my head
I squirm, I wiggle and move about
Then finally I crawl out of bed.

I mosey over to the bedroom window
Take hold of the shade and look outside
The sun is shining, it's a beautiful day
I thought as I drew a big sigh.

Good morning world! Hello Jesus!
It's gonna be a great day, I see
I have so much to do, so many plans
Will you walk along with me?

Because you see I know from days gone by
There's nothing the two of us can't do
But help me Lord in all my plans
It might all be pleasing with you.

Well, it's been a long day, we've worked very hard
Every task we undertook is done
It's such a good feeling to have company you know
And together we did have fun

Now as I slowly kneel and bow my head
We'll just have a talk together
Then very tiredly I'll climb into bed
Close one eye—then the other.

Ain't God Good to All Us Christians

Ain't God good to all us Christians
Ain't He people, ain't He tho?
From the very pretty and youngest
To the feeble who are old
Ain't God good to all us Christians
Ain't He people, ain't He tho?
From the break of dawn in morning
Till the dusk creeps in at night
As He gives us lips to speak with
Nose to smell and eyes for sight
Hands to feel with, feet to walk on
Strength to do the work we must
A mind to think with, wisdom with it
Patience with those who cause a fuss
Ain't God good to all us Christians
Ain't He people, ain't He tho?
With a home, a church to go to
Clothes to wear, shoes on our feet
Never, ever get real hungry
We have plenty food to eat
A nice car to ride around in
Money for the things we really need
Never really want for nothing
Tis a comfy life we lead
Paying the debt for all our sins
So that we might not be lost
He sent His son to this old earth
And there He died upon the cross
No greater love hath any man
On earth or in heaven above
No greater gift can anyone give
Than the gift of God's great love
From the very pretty and youngest
To the feeble who are old
Ain't God good to all us Christians
Ain't He people, ain't He tho?
As He guides our every footstep
Sends us blessings, yea untold.

Can You Believe?

Can you believe that Jesus came to earth
Just to lead and guide us along the way?
Can you believe that Jesus walked
On earth, just as you do today?
Can you believe that Jesus talked to
People on earth that He loved so much?
Can you believe Jesus preached God's word
To sinners just like us?
Can you believe Jesus ate earthly food
While here—with His fellow man?
Can you believe that Jesus walked, talked,
And preached throughout all the land?
Can you believe that people just like us
Saw, believed and tried to do what He said?
Jesus loves us, He can be our personal
Saviour, if we'll just follow where He has led.

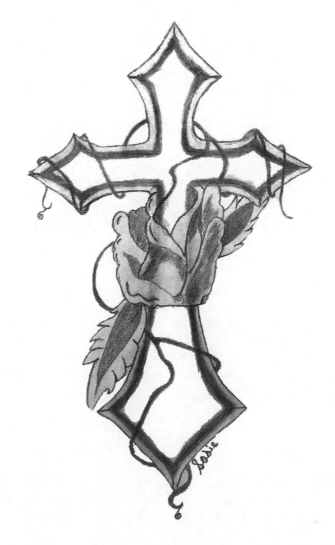

Converted

I've been converted
I've been made whole
I've been converted
God saved my soul
May I strive always
Worthy to be
I've been converted
God set me free.

Crucifixion

At the foot of the Mount of Olives
In the garden called Gethsemane
Christ Jesus, our Savior knelt in prayer
And there He prayed, tho in great pain and agony
"Oh, Father I know all things are possible
So, have mercy, take away this cup from me,
Nevertheless not my will but thine
Is what I ask just now of Thee."
Being in agony He prayed more earnestly
With no friends or family around
And the sweat He sweat were as drops of blood
As He knelt there on the ground
The people in that day found Him guilty
They said, "He must surely die."
His blood may be upon us and our children
For this man we must crucify.
They stripped Him of all of His clothing
And put upon Him a robe of bright red
A crown of thorns they platted for Jesus
And placed them firmly upon His head.
A reed they placed in His right hand
And very few of the people even knew
That as they mocked and spit upon this man
It was "Jesus, King of the Jews"
They took wooden poles tied them together
And compelled Simeon, a man from Cyrene
To carry the cross up Golgotha Hill
The soldiers were so brazen and so mean
Nails they drove through His hands and feet
And in His side a spear they did sink
They gave Him vinegar, mingled with gall
He tasted, but He wouldn't drink
They cast lots and divided his garments
For all the people who were there to see
And about the ninth hour He cried out loud,
"My God, my God, why hast Thou forsaken me?"
No one knew the shame or agony
Of this Jew from Galilee
Who suffered on the cross on Golgotha Hill
For the people of the world to see.
As He hung on the cross His head bent low
His eyelids closed as if in deep sleep
Blood was running down His cheeks from thorns
On His head; over His quiet lips did creep
The pain was so great it was beyond compare
And again in a very loud voice He cried
There on the cross, Jesus shed His blood for you and for me
And He gave up the Ghost and died.

Did You Ever Stop To Wonder

Did you ever stop to wonder
How a snake could crawl so low
How a giraffe could be so tall
How a turtle could crawl so slow?

Did you ever stop to wonder
How the grass could be so green
How the trees could lose their leaves
How the flowers could bloom in Spring?

Did you ever stop to wonder
How the valleys could be so low
How the mountains could be so high
How the rivers always flow?

Did you ever stop to wonder
How the Heavens cry their rain
How the sun shines with a smile
How it snows and sleets in pain?

Did you ever stop to wonder
How the stars light up the sky
How the thunder rolls in anger
How the lightning flashes by?

Did you ever stop to wonder
About all these wonders of man
It took a supreme architect
Only God could lay the plan.

Do You Believe In Jesus?

Do you believe in Jesus?
Was the question asked that day
To all the people passing by as they hurried on their way
Some folks smiled, then began to giggle
And some murmured in dismay
Some just whispered among themselves
While others simply had nothing to say
But one little man stood all alone
His head was bent down low
He raised his head then firmly replied
I'll tell you what I know
No, I don't believe in Jesus
And what's more, I never have
But I've been taught about Jesus
Since I was a tiny lad,
Mamma used to tell me Bible stories
As I cuddled upon her lap
And she rocked me sound asleep
For my daily daytime nap
The story of the baby Moses
How in a basket among the reeds
He was saved from Pharaoh the evil king
With all his hate and greed
And Elijah, the great Bible prophet
Who was spared the sting of death
Went to Heaven in a chariot of fire
To dwell with God and the blessed
Then as a silly young teenager
I learned how God would guide
My talk, my actions, and my innermost thoughts
If on him I only relied
So you see, I don't believe in Jesus
I know Him, He's my friend
And to have a friend like Jesus
Means that life will have no end.

God Answers Prayer

If you kneel down by your bed
And you bow your humble head
God will listen whether night or day
If you mean it every word
Then you know that God has heard
God will answer every prayer you pray.

If you don't want to live in sin
Ask God to cleanse your heart within
God will listen whether night or day
All your burden He will bear
All your joys and comforts share
God will hear every prayer you pray.

Won't you say a little prayer
Just to let God know you care
God will listen whether night or day
Won't you thank the Lord somehow
For all the blessings you have now
God will listen every time you pray.

Chorus

God answers prayer—I know He does
He answers prayer—I know He does
God will answer every prayer you pray
God answers prayer—I know He does
He answers prayer—I know He does
I know because He answered them for me.

Written in 1941.

God Will Never Forget His Children

God will never forget His children
He will guide them everyday
Over trials and temptations
He'll go with them all the way

God will never forget His children
Nor will he let them go astray
If they pray to Him in earnest
And talk with Him each day

God will never forget His children
When they're in sorrow, happy, or gay
If they just remember their Saviour
He'll restore their soul away

God will never forget His children
Hasn't He proven that to you
When you went to Him for favors
And lived faithful, honest, and true.

Written 1942.

He Gave

He gave me feet to walk on
He gave me hands to feel
He gave me ears to hear with
He gave me lips to speak
He gave me eyes to see
All this God gave to me.

He gave me health to do
He gave me mind to reason
He gave me love to share with others
He gave me wisdom to know
He gave me peace within
But what have I given Him?

Help

Help me to be a better Christian
Have fun, be jolly, be gay
Help me to be a better Christian
Help me, Lord, I pray
Help me to be a better Christian
As I journey along life's way
Help me Lord to be a better Christian
As I live from day to day.

Help Me!

Oh Lord there must be thousands
Tonight who are out in sin
Help me to speak of Jesus
Help me to guide them in
Help me to be a friend
To strangers I might meet
Help me to shake their hand
When I meet them on the street
Help me to show them kindness
In everything I do
Help me to show them patience
And have mercy on them too
Help me Lord to love them
And let them know I care
Help me to teach them Jesus
Anytime, anyplace, anywhere

How Long Has It Been?

How long has it been since you talked with your Maker?
He really cares for you—you know that—you must
But He knows in your weakness you can be blown away with a breath
You're fragile, like flowers, or a big cloud of dust.

How long has it been since you prayed to your Father?
And asked Him for patience, wisdom, and love
Asked Him to lead you, to guide you, and direct you
Then ask for His mercy and forgiveness from above.

How long has it been since you thanked God for His blessings?
And thanked Him for giving His life on the cross
And for taking your sins as far as the Heaven's above you
So that your soul might be saved and not lost.

How long has it been since you told God you loved Him?
With every fiber of your body and soul
From the very depths of your feelings and innate
With everything that makes your body whole

So pause, take a few minutes and talk with your Maker
Pray earnestly to your Heavenly Father above
Thank Him for all He has done—is doing—or ever will do
But most of all—let God know just how much He is loved.

I've Got A Dream—A Vision

I've got a dream—a vision
Tis a big dream for little ol' me
A black limozine, shiny and fair
A silver plane that flies through the air
A big yacht that glides o'er the waves
A motorcycle to shimmy and sway
Acres of land, full of oil for to drill
A huge castle set high on a hill
Fancy clothes with buttons and bows
Pretty shoes with bright colored hose
The glitter of silver and of gold
All the money that life can unfold
No—none of these
But I've got a dream—a vision
It's as tho through a dark glass I see
Tis a mansion, it's far, far away
And if I get there, forever I'll stay
Tis a beautiful home, there's none can compare
It has bright colored lights, gold everywhere
The glitter and glamour—it's a sight to behold
And the love of the angels never grows old
Joy, peace, contentment all these I faintly see
Just imagine! God prepared all this for little ol' me
Yes, I've got a dream—a vision
Someday, with God's grace, very clearly I will see.

Jesus

Baby Jesus
With guardian angels
Was sent to Mary and Joseph that day
Baby Jesus
Born in a manger
With a bed made out of hay
Baby Jesus
In all His glory
Was wrapped in swaddling clothes of old
Baby Jesus
Son of God
The greatest story ever told.

Jesus

Jesus, Son of God surrounded by angels
Sent to earth by virgin birth
To grow up in a world of sin
To walk among men
To preach and teach the gospel
To die on the cross
To be resurrected from the dead
To live again
To organize His church
To ascend to Heaven
To prepare a mansion
That through His love, mercy, and grace
There we might be also
All of this He did for you and me
And we continue to go the way of the world
And say no to Him who gave so much W-H-Y?

Jesus

The words he softly spoke
He spoke for me
The careful steps He took
He took for me
Each thoughtful deed He did
He did for me
Each drop of blood he shed
He shed for me
When He died on Calvary
He died for me.

Each word I speak
I must speak softly for Him
Each step I take
I must take for Him
Each deed I do
I must do for Him
Every day of my life
I must live for Him
And if I am asked
(God give me the strength)
And let me die for Him.

Joe

Tears running down his dirty little cheeks
Joe sat on the curb all by himself
Oh! How it hurt to sit there all alone
But his friends had all gone someplace else
They said they were going to Sunday school
Boy! That must be some place grand
They talked about Jesus and how He loved everyone
But Joe just didn't quite understand
He sat there a while, with his mind wandering round
Then he jumped up and took off in a run
He thought, "Mom can tell me about Sunday School
And why the kids have so much fun"
Please—Mom—please let's go to Sunday School
The kids on the street have all gone
But Mom scarcely heard what little Joe said
She kept right on working singing her song.
Sunday after Sunday they packed a lunch
And went to the beach for the day
They swam, fished, went riding in a boat
And lots of water games they learned to play
Ever so swiftly the years went by
Little Joe was growing up very fast
Tho he never mentioned it ever again
Sometimes his mind wandered back to the past
But only for a moment would he let himself think
Of the kids who all played on the street
For each had grown up and gone their separate ways
Sometimes he wondered if they ever again would meet
But Joe had no time to think about the past
He was having so much fun living today
He had a big night planned with all the gang
So he had to get started right away
The hours went by and day light came
Mamma peeked in Joe's room just to see
If Joe was snuggled down in his bed
But Joes wasn't where he should be
Then Mamma heard a noise, a shuffle, and a thud
And she ran to open the door
There laid Joe, all weary and worn
Curled up and passed out on the floor
Mamma covered him up to keep him good and warm
Her little baby such a short time ago
Where have I failed—where did I go wrong?
But somehow—she just didn't know
Joe opened his eyes—Mamma was still sitting there
On her little ol' kitchen stool
Why Joe? She said—Why?
His weary reply "If only you had taken me to Sunday School"

I Love Jesus

I love Jesus
I talk with Him each day
I love Jesus
I work, I serve, I pray
I love Jesus
A better Christian I hope to be
If you love Jesus
Come along with me.

I Thank The Lord Jesus

For dying on the cross for me
For giving me a chance for Eternal Life
For loving me in all my sin
For giving me Christian parents
For leading me to a Christian husband
For giving my children a Christian Daddy
For loaning me eight beautiful, healthy children
For food, shelter, and clothing
For teaching me to love my fellow man
For helping me to be ever humble in thy sight
I Thank Thee Lord Jesus

Life-Candle

Life is like a candle when you light it, the flame leaps high.

It is likened unto a new born babe when it pops into this big wide wonderful world.

A new life is begun as the flame glows.

The wick grows shorter as it continues to burn day after day.

So is life as it begins to ebb and journeys down that long and lonely pathway.

The wick travels slowly down the center of the candle.

So as our life travels down that straight and narrow pathway towards our journeys end.

As it gets closer to the bottom it burns slower and slower.

The light grows dimmer and dimmer as we near the end.

Our movements get slower and slower – we're tired, weary.

Finally the light flickers, flickers again and quietly goes out.

As it has burned to the end of the wax the wick is done.

So we too dragging our feet, mind, and eyes failing begin to murmur and whisper.

Finally a flutter of the eye and a wave of the hand, it's the end of the candle of life.

We find rest, sweet rest, sweet peace as we shake hands with Jesus.

*Illustrated with love
by the family of Rowlen Reason
Billie
Joshua, Tara
Annah, Cadie, Trinity
Jenni, Everett
& Brock*

125

Mercy

Love me Jesus—love me Jesus
I'm just a mold of clay made with mighty hands
Love me Jesus—love me Jesus
Only love like yours could ever understand

Help me Jesus—help me Jesus
Help me to do the things I know you want me to
Help me Jesus—help me Jesus
Help me to live a life that's pleasing to you

Forgive me Jesus—forgive me Jesus
Forgive me for the sins I have committed against Thee
Forgive me Jesus—forgive me Jesus
Forgive and let me live with you throughout eternity.

My Jesus

This is a story that never grows old,
A story that's so often been told,
Of a man so courageous and bold,
My Jesus

Let this cup pass from me,
This was Jesus prayerful plea,
As He knelt there on His knees,
My Jesus

Said the people can't you see,
He's as guilty as can be,
So let's hang Him on a tree,
My Jesus

Up the hill His cross He bore,
And His feet were tired and sore,
He called upon His God once more,
My Jesus

The thorns they placed upon His head,
The blood upon His cheeks was red,
It was just as God had said,
My Jesus

There He hung upon the tree,
For the whole wide world to see,
To save a sinner such as me,
My Jesus

My Friend

Just as the night broke into day
The stars in the sky went skipping away
I heard a knock—there--I heard it again
So I went to the door to let Him in
He was no stranger-no siree
He had been a friend for years to me
But I was just taken so by surprise
I just couldn't quite realize
Why? At this early hour of the day
My Friend would be passing along this way
He wasn't just passing, He made that quite clear
With our close communication He was already near
For you see the hour of time doesn't matter to Him
He knew I was troubled, so He just dropped in
We sat down in the wee hours of the day
We had so much to discuss, so much to say
We talked about the joys and blessings in life
Then we discussed the troubles, heartaches, and strife
It all seemed so easy with Him there to help
I didn't have it all to figure out by myself
Because this Friend who was here-right here by my side
He was with me all those days and nights when I had cried
I was so glad my Friend just dropped in
Because now I can unload my burdens on Him
You see this Friend is much bigger than I
He can carry the burdens where I only try
Now I have peace and joy within my heart
The whole wide world can't tear it apart
The time so swiftly had just slipped by
My Friend stood up—He was saying goodbye
Oh! How I hated to see Him move toward the door
I was so afraid I wouldn't see Him any more
And it was so much easier to talk to Him here
Than to try and reach Him on a line of prayers
But with a wave of my hand, I bid Him adieu
As my Friend slipped through the door and faded from view

My Friend Named Jesus

I was a sad and lonely sinner
Living a life of sin
Till I heard of someone
Who could change my heart within
Then I met a friend named Jesus
I only met Him today
I met a friend named Jesus
I met Him when I knelt to pray.

Now He will guide my footsteps
And my hands each day
He will help me speak
And know just what to say
For I have a friend named Jesus
I only met Him today
Yes, I have a friend named Jesus
I met Him when I knelt to pray

The rest of my life I will serve Him
Shouting His praises to all
Praying each one will accept Him
Please won't you answer His call
If you haven't met my friend, Jesus
I want you to meet Him today.
Come meet my friend named Jesus
As we kneel down and pray

My Prayer

Help me say what I should say
Help me speak of Thee each day
Help me be a better Christian than before
If I stutter and grow weak
Give me strength and clear my speech
Help me be a better Christian day by day.

Help me walk along life's way
Guide my steps from day to day
Help me be a better Christian than before
If I stumble please understand
If I fall, Lord, take my hand
Help me be a better Christian day by day.

A home in Heaven is my goal
Lord have mercy, save my soul
Let me live in Heaven, Dear Lord, I pray with Thee
When my life on earth is o'er
Lord, let me live forever more
Let me live with Thee throughout Eternity.

Neath The Shadow Of The Cross

Neath the shadow of the cross there goes Simon of Cyrene
Carrying the cross for Jesus up the hill
His load was heavy, his grief was great
But the law of prophecy he must help to fulfill.

Neath the shadow of the cross there stands Peter
As if in a daze, his head bent low
Three times, very clearly, he denied Jesus
Just as Jesus had said, it was so.

Neath the shadow of the cross we find Judas
With bewilderment written on his face
Why? Why? For just 30 pieces of shiny silver
He betrayed Jesus, in shame and disgrace.

Neath the shadow of the cross we see Pilate
Confused in turmoil at what they asked him to do
He knew in his heart Jesus was innocent
So he said, "I wash my hands, now it's up to you."

There upon the cross hangs my Jesus
Bearing the pain and agony for you and me
Thorns pierced his head, a sword pierced his side
The nails driven in his hands were plain to see.

Neath the shadow of the cross there sits Mary
Quiet and mournful, watching Jesus, her beloved Son
As his eyes closed and his lips stood still
She knew ---His battle at last was won!

Red Quarry

Red Quarry is really becoming quite famous, you know
As it sits out here on the hill
For all its confusion, babies crying, children laughing
(Sometimes whispering) they just can't be still

But I just wish each one of you could have
Spent these past two weeks with us
And watched these children as they listened,
Learned, read and then discussed

The Bible and the teachings of Jesus
And the things he wants them to do
The way He wants them to live
All their whole life through

I wish each morning you could have seen
Their sleepy little eyes
And later the big happy grins on their faces
I wish you could have heard their voices

As they rang out loud and clear
For they love to sing God's praises
They like to be in the little church programs
Or maybe play in the children's band

They're usually ready and willing
To help in any way they can
So you see God has sent us "showers of blessings"
He has filled our church full of children

In Isaiah C.11 Verse 6: God tells us
A little child shall lead them.

Sacrifice of Abraham

God had a talk with Abraham
Back in Bible days of old
He told him to go to Mariah
And this is how the story goes

Abraham arose, very early one morning
Saddled his ass and they were ready to go
He took two very young men with him
And Isaac, his son, went also

He took special wood for a burnt offering
And went to the place God had said
They rode three days before lifting their eyes
To see the place where God had led

And Abraham said to the two young men
Abide ye here with the ass
While we go yonder for to worship
Just me and the young lad

Abraham took the wood for the burnt offering
And gave it to Isaac, for to carry
He took the fire in his hand and a knife
And said, "Come, we must not tarry."

And Isaac said to Abraham, his father
"Behold, the fire and the wood is at hand
But where is the lamb for the offering?"
Abraham knew Isaac wouldn't understand

They came to the place where God had told them
And Abraham built an altar so fair
He laid all the wood in perfect order
Bound his son and placed him there

And as Abraham stretched forth his hand
And took the knife to slay his son
The angel of the Lord called unto him
And said, "Halt, your mission is done."

The angel said, "Lay not thy hand upon this lad.
Neither do any harm unto your son
For now I know that thou do fearest God
And would sacrifice your only son."

And Abraham, weary, from all he'd been through
Lifted his eyes, looked around and behold

133

Tangled in a thicket, caught by his horns
A beautiful ram that had strayed from the fold

Abraham offered the ram for the burnt offering
Upon the altar where the wood was laid
His only son had just been spared
Because the hand of Abraham God had stayed

Senses

Eyes cannot see
Nose cannot smell
Ears cannot hear
Lips cannot tell
Of the beauties of Heaven
The scents of the air
The harps of the angels
God went to prepare

Thanks

"Thanks" seems like such a little word
But its meaning has endless bounds
For all the things that God supplies
For all of us—just look around
Streams that flow with water so blue
Fish that swim in the deep
Birds that sing at the break of dawn
And crickets that chirp us to sleep
Trees that bud in Spring; so pretty and green
Wild flowers blooming in the fields
Pastures all green with grass on the hillsides
And crops that grow tall and yield
Food on the table to supply our needs
Clothing to wear to keep us warm
Protection and help we have at our call
To keep us from evil or harm
But more than all of these Christ died for us
As He shed His blood on the cross
He gave us a chance for Eternal life
And He wanted not one soul to be lost
So you see we have so much to be thankful for
As this Thanksgiving Day rolls around
"Thanks" seems like such a little word
But its meaning has endless bounds

The Bible

It all started out many years ago
When they took sharp tools one by one
And carved on tablets of smooth soft clay
Then let it dry in the bright hot sun.

Then they killed the animals for their skins
Sewed them in great long lengths
Prepared the surface quite clean and smooth
And wrote the message, by hand, in ink

Then we had papyrus from far away Egypt
Which was made from inexpensive reeds
It was made into sheets and rolled into scrolls
But was sometimes very hard to read

It took so much time and trouble to write
That only a few Bibles were written
They were so expensive, only the rich could afford
To have one in their possession

Then in 1450 printing was invented
And Bibles were much less expensive
Now most every home has a Bible within
And the word of God is most impressive

So now you see why the Bible is such a precious book
It took lots of time, patience, and skill
Do you have a Bible? Do you read it and live it?
Do you try to do God's will?

The Birth of Jesus

Long, long time ago in a faraway land
Lived Mary, a woman, and Joseph, a man
Mary was with child of the Holy Ghost
But she was not married so she dare not boast
Joseph was minded to hide her away
On these thoughts he prayed and he pondered day after day
Then God sent a message by an angel in a dream
He told Joseph, "Things are not really as bad as they seem."
So be not afraid, take Mary to be thy wife
Love her, cherish her, you'll have a good life
For unto you shall be born a wonderful son
You shall call Him Jesus—"The Holy One"
So Joseph took Mary and went to Galilee
A new life for the two it was going to be
The days passed slowly, one by one
As the two of them waited for their new son
Caesar Augustus said, "There are taxes to pay."
So Mary and Joseph had to be on their way
To the city of Bethlehem they set out to go
Mary was with child so they traveled slow
Mary rode the donkey, the road way was rough
As for food and water—they took just enough
When they arrived—there was no place to stay
Except in a barn full of cattle and hay
While they were there Mary's time had come
And Mary delivered her first born, a son
There was just no room for Him in the Inn
They had no clothes to dress Him in
So in a manger piled full of hay
Wrapped in swaddling clothes, Mary's baby lay
Twas a lowly birth this Baby had
But it was no dream or myth or fad
It was just as God said that it would be
He sent a Saviour to the world to save you and me

The Bridge

We are facing a bridge—we all must cross it
There's none other like it on earth
We begin to walk it and continue on our way
From the day God gives us birth
It's a long journey—no one has said it was easy
Sometimes we almost lose our way
For we have burdens, sorrows, and struggles galore
But we must keep on fighting day after day
Now let's look at this bridge that we all must cross
It goes from earth to Heaven, you see?
God gave us the Bible as a map for this bridge
And He said, "Come follow me."
Now God's the greatest leader we could have
We can't cross this bridge without Him
So if we want to cross this bridge from earth to Heaven
We all must work—hard—without a whimper or whim

The Little White Church On The Hill

On a crooked road way out in the country
High upon a beautiful hill
At the edge of the woods, sits a little white church
Ever so quiet—ever so still
It's really a very old, old building
And it's set right here for years
In its walls it holds many memories
Some are happy, some filled with tears
These great big doors are always open
And they say "Welcome, come on in."
Free your heart of all its troubles
All your sorrows—all your sins
This little, old white church house
Has been good to me and mine
As we come out here each Sunday
Seldom ever make it right on time
It has helped us raise our family
In a Christian—loving home
As we've taught them God's way of living
Then one by one, they've gone out on their own
We have come here and sung our "specials"
Not for man, but for God above
And you folk just sit and listened
Because your hearts were filled with love
Sunday after Sunday—here I stood
And my poetry I have read
Some was good---some not so good
Anyway that's what good folk said
We have mingled with our Christian
Neighbors and friends we know they're dear
We have had some wonderful preachers
Who have come from far and near
In this quiet, still place, I can meet my Jesus
I am sure to always find Him here
I can come here and sing His praises
Or kneel and talk with him in prayer
It's a place where I can come and study
All the things He wants me to
And then He'll go and walk beside me
As I meet the world—His will to do
All of this is good my friends and neighbors
God has blessed us so richly from above
So may we continue to share our Christian living
Our hope, our faith, and our love

The Love Of God

Paul and Silas were preaching about Jesus
There was an angry mob milling round
They did not like the message they were hearing
And great fear was much profound
The magistrates laid many stripes upon Paul and Silas
They tore their clothes off and threw them down
They cast Paul and Silas into the inner prison
And there—their feet were bound
But along about midnight Paul and Silas
Began to sing spiritual hymns of praise
The prisoner's ears were receptive
As they heard the prayers that were prayed
But suddenly! There was a great earthquake
And the bands that bound their feet
Were loosed and the doors of the prison opened
Their freedom they now could seek
Immediately the keeper of the prison
Was awakened from his sleep
Supposing the prisoners had escaped
He surely must have weeped
Then he drew his sword to kill himself
But Paul cried, "Do thyself no harm."
The prisoners were safe within the walls
There was no need for alarm
Trembling—the keeper fell down before Paul and Silas
And said, "Sirs, what must I do to be saved?"
For this night he had witnessed the power of God
And now a Christian life he craved
So you see folks we as sinners
Can humbly ask ourselves today
Just like the Philippian jailor
"What must I do to be saved?"
God has given all of us the answer
It's just as plain and simple as can be
Believe, repent, confess, and be baptized
For God's love found a pardon for you and me

The Resurrection

On the first day of the week in the early dawn
There was a great earthquake—all the land o'er
An angel of the Lord descended from Heaven
And rolled back the stone away from the door
The angel's countenance was just like lightening
The raiment was white as if it were snow
All the knowledge of this great incident
Was not revealed for man to know
The keeper's eyes showed their amazement
Their bodies shook great with fear
They lay as if they were dead men
As the angel of God hovered near
Mary Magdalene and the other Mary
Came to the tomb where Jesus lay
They stood as if they were paralyzed
And had not one word to say
The angel said unto the women
"Fear not, for I know why you come
You come to seek Jesus your Saviour
Who was crucified for each and everyone
But He is not here—He is risen
Come—see the place where He lay
Go quickly, tell all His disciples."
Behold! Whom should they see
But Jesus the Saviour who had been crucified
King of the Jews from Galilee
"All hail—Be not afraid"
This was what the Master said
They held His feet and worshipped Him
Their Lord had risen from the dead
Yes, He arose from the dead for you and for me
By His grace, our sins He forgives
He arose in victory o'er death and the grave
And thank God, today our Jesus lives.

Matthew 28:1-10

We Taught You

Love-
> Love is the key to the kingdom

Jesus said-
> Faith, hope, and charity, but the greatest of these is love

Honesty-
> Truth and fairness to your fellow man

Kindness-
> Is gentleness and courtesy to all

Joy-
> Gives you laughter and happiness

Wisdom-
> Gives courage and the will to do

But most of all we showed you a map for eternal life
Don't lose it, use it for therein you will find peace
Contentment and life everlasting

Will That Make A Christian Out Of Me?

If I go to church each Sunday
If I say that I believe
If I confess all of my sins
Will that make a Christian out of me?

If I repent and say I'm sorry
If I'm baptized so others may see
If I praise His name in public
Will that make a Christian out of me?

If I pray sincere prayers for others
If I sing praises unto Thee
If I proclaim Thy name is Holy
Will that make a Christian out of me?

If a good and Godly life I liveth
If I communicate daily with Thee
If love pours from my heart freely
Will that make a Christian out of me?

All these things Jesus has commanded
He said, "Do these if you love me."
And if I do as Jesus has commanded
It will surely make a Christian out of me.

Would You Think That God Was Near?

When you tell those little stories
When your neighbors you do sneer
When you go around and gossip
Would you think that God was near?

When you go to some old roadhouse
When you drink a glass of beer
When you sit parked along the roadside
Would you think that God was near?

Won't you read the Holy Bible?
Won't you pray till you know God hears?
For if you want to enter Heaven
You must know that God is near!

CATEGORY

12

SAD

Prisoner

In this dark and dismal cell
With cobwebs hanging low
With rats and mice playing around
Tickling my feet as they go
No food or water have I had
Nor can my friends come near
No soft and low sweet music
From the radio can I hear
The judge pronounced my sentence
And to death I must go
For a crime I haven't committed
But they won't believe it's so
I can hear the death bells warning
As it rings out loud and clear
I can hear the guards marching along
My time is drawing near.

Bridget Lo

It was in the fall of the year
The lazy wind was swaying the trees
When Bridget Lo drove off in a car
A sparkling brunette at age twenty-three
Her lips wore a smile for everyone
Her kindness was just plain to see
Her deep blue eyes just danced with joy
She was happy, jolly, and free
A very light drizzle began to fall
And her car, at a high rate of speed
Rounded a curve, slid to and fro
Went off the road, straight into a tree
Those deep blue eyes that once danced with joy
For the brunette at age twenty-three
Would never again tell night from day
For Bridget Lo could no longer see.

Cloud Of No Return

One by one they are saying goodbye
Vanishing into a white fluffy cloud that turns
It's a misty cloud—I cannot see through
But it's a cloud of no return

Is the road straight or crooked, I do not know
Is it rough or easy, I cannot say
Neither do I know whom they will meet
When they get to the end of the way

But this I know, life here is o'er
This old world they leave behind
I know not where or what their fate
But a whole new world they will find

Another dear one just waved goodbye
From a white fluffy cloud that turns
It's a misty cloud—I cannot see through
But I know, it's a cloud that won't return

Cry

This morning I kissed him as he left for work
With a great big smile I waved goodbye
I watched his car slowly move away, down the long narrow road
Then I cried.

This afternoon, I patted his cheeks, ruffled his hair
My rosy cheeked son and then I tried
To laugh, joke, and be happy but all the while, somehow I knew
Then I cried.

Tonight, I brushed her hair, hugged her tight
And sent her upstairs with a sigh to say her prayers
Jump into her bed snuggle down under the cover, warm and cozy
Then I cried.

I had already fainted, went blind temporarily,
For some time now I knew I was quite ill
And would soon die, so now here I sit in this big old house
All alone, nothing to do but think
And so I cry.

Deep, Down, Dark, Despair

These few words express my feelings
On a lonely night like this
No caressing arms to hold me
Not even a warm goodnight kiss
No one here to share my prayers with
Or to hold my hand in his
No one to whisper sweet words of nothing
That was music to my ears
How I need your strength to lift me
Wisdom to guide me in the night
Patience to show me what to do
Comfort you gave night after night
Deep, down, dark, despair
How my heart aches for you tonight
Can you see me? Can you hear me?
Please tell me everything's alright.

Depth

Deep is my sorrow
Lost in the shadow of light
Wandering in darkness
Black as the night.

I cannot see any future
Life has no meaning for me
My heart—Oh!—my heart is heavy
My burdens won't let me be.

Despair is a turmoil
No way can I explain
The depth of my agony
Feelings of grief, heartache, and pain.

The load is far too heavy
I cannot carry it—not me
I need strength from the Master
Jesus, He knows and can set me free.

Life

From whence I come I do not know
But into somebody's home I go
To bring a lot of happiness and joy
As do all little girls and boys
Then as I grow, I'm off to school
Can't grow up and be somebody's fool
A lot of books—to home I bring
To learn of this and that and everything
A teenager I soon become
I think my life has just begun
Then I find another to take as my mate
I learn to love instead of hate
We have a family and make a home
One was not meant to live alone
I work so hard for my silver and gold
And all the wealth I can manage to hold
Power—more power I gain thro the years
My vanity grows, I've nothing to fear
I have mansions, the finest by far
I have airplanes, boats, and cars
I wine and dine with the wealthy, the great
I want to live a little before it's too late
The years pass by so fast it seems
But I've accomplished all my dreams
The children have married—gone from the nest
It's time to retire and take a rest
The days pass swiftly now one by one
I begin to wonder from whence I come
Have I lived my life all in vain
Could I do better if I lived it again
Questions, questions but no answers I find
Confusion and turmoil crowd my mind
As my health fades and life grows dim
There's no peace or contentment within
I'll go to my grave and never know
From whence I come or where I'll go
Because while here, you see, I failed to find
The Master, the Maker of all mankind

Little Ol' Me

I'm tormented—I'm flustrated
I'm really a mess
Just don't know anything to do
But simply confess

My head is spinning
Can't get it to stop
It keeps getting bigger and bigger
Feels like it's gonna pop

I don't see very well
My visions a blur
My lips are a quiver
My speech is a slur

My ears are stopped up
Can't seem to hear
My nose lost its smeller
I sadly fear

These are all major problems
And I'm just one little ol' me
Please won't you give back
All you've taken from me

I wanta live my life freely
Be healthy, happy, and free
So torment and flustration
You get away from me!

Lonely?

Lonely—just a six letter word
Do you know what it means
Did you ever set in a building filled with people
No one knew you were there
Did anyone really care
Did you ever live in a home with a big family
Lonely—but did anyone see
Did you ever try to talk to your parents
You just couldn't get across that bridge
Lonely—was this six letter word just wrote for me
Does anyone care
Can anyone see
Lonely—I know what it means—that's me

Look Inside

If you could only look inside
Of this old frame—called me
And watch the fight day after day
And see the things I see

If you could only look inside
And see the darkness there
Watch the troubled waters flow
Through my veins in deep despair

If you could only look inside
And watch my spirit fight
Through all the confusion and turmoil
For just a glimpse of light

If you could only look inside
Watch the devils tear me apart
Drag my soul to the depths of hell
And crucify my heart

If you could only look inside
See all the rips, jags, and tears
Would you help me? Could you help me?
Or would you even care?

No one to assure me everything's all right

No one to turn out the light

No one to discuss the toils of the day

No one to hold hands and pray

No one to warm my bed

No arm to cradle my head

No arms to hold me tight

No lips to kiss goodnight

Emptiness is all I feel

Yet I know that life's for real

No I don't wonder why I can't sleep

Yes, I know why I lay and weep

O'er

Down on my knees, arms outstretched
Hair hanging down, head bent o'er
Tears streaming down my tired, weary face
I whispered, please, I love you so
But with a grin on your face, a twinkle in your eye
You shrugged your shoulders and turned to go
I knew right then as my heart stood still
And my body crumbled in anguish and woe
I knew that life on earth for the two of us together was already o'er
The happiness, joy, and laughter we had shared
Was gone for us forevermore

Special Secret

On a cold dreary night
As black as could be
Fog had settled in
And we could hardly see
We rounded a curve
Left the road, hit a tree
When I came to
I was crawling on my knees
My toes and fingers were numb
Black was all I could see
But little did I know
That's how it would always be
The sirens were buzzing
People were gathering 'round
But there I lay so numb
On the hard, cold ground
They put me on a stretcher
Wrapped me up good and warm
Told me everything was alright
Not to be alarmed
They held my hand
Soothed ways my fears
Brushed my hair from my forehead
Wiped away all my tears
The days I spent in the hospital
Seemed so long and drear
The friends that came to visit
Were very dear
After many, many days
Of agony and pain
I was released to come home
But I would never see again
With family and friends all around me
The days passed by
Sometimes I laughed
But sometimes I cried
Tho now I am totally blind
Still I can plainly see
All the love in your heart
You still have for me
And my love for you
Will never grow old
Our love for each other is gentle but bold
So we'll keep our little secret
Just me and you
It will always be special the love between us two

The Ole Swimming Hole

It was a beautiful day in summer
The sun was shining bright
The grass was green, flowers in bloom
There was a swimming party that night
The young folks were running in and out
Getting their hot dogs and buns
They deviled the eggs, made potato salad
They were going to have lots of fun
After a hayride down the ole country road
They ate their fill for the day
They jumped into their bathing suits
And they were on their way
Just over the hill to the ole swimming hole
They laughed and joked together
When they reached the bank they dived right in
First one and then the other
A yell for help they all could hear
And turned in Jan's direction
Only to see her sink fast away
There was no one there for protection
She couldn't swim said Joe her friend
But she didn't want anyone to know
I tried to catch her and pull her back
But I guess I was just too slow
Joe just stood there ever so helpless
His arms hung limp at his sides
Tears were running down his cheeks
Because the girl he loved just died

CATEGORY

13

SERIOUS

Secrets

May the secrets that I hold within my heart
In this life never be revealed
May my mouth be closed in silence
And my lips forever sealed

May no one ever guess or know
The heartache that I feel
For life must go on in its dreams and myths
Thank God I know He's real

Tired

Tired—do you really know what it means?
Can you express it? Or explain it?
Tired—Oh! The weariness
The numbness of the muscles—the aching of the bones
Blurred vision—the flightiness of mind
Tired—do you know what it means?
It's me—at the close of a hard day's work

CATEGORY

14

THOUGHTFUL

Dusk to Twilight

From the dusk of evening to twilight of morn
Tis time for a person to put all cares away
Time for worries of the mind to cease
Time for labors of a long day to halt
And tensions of the physical body release

From the dusk of evening to twilight of morn
Tis a peaceful, quiet time in a person's life
A relaxing time for both body and soul
To pause and rest for renewal and strength
Because another hard day has taken its toll

I Saw A Man

I saw a man the other day
His hair was long, dirty, and tangled and grey
His eyes looked sad, then I saw a tear
His face wore the expression of sadness and fear
His hands were all greasy and grimy with dirt
His nails were split, hands cracked, they hurt
His clothes were so dirty, wrinkled and torn
The odor they had, said how long they'd been worn
His shoes were scuffed, with a hole here and there
There was no doubt he could use a new pair
He sat around town day after day
With the rest of his friends just chattin' away
Telling each other about their bad luck in life
Crying the blues of heartache and strife
Maybe he would find a little food for the day
Just enough to keep starvation away
This man's life is so sad but true
Will the life of this man reflect in you?
Then I saw another man the other day
His hair was short, thinning, and grey
His eyes had a twinkle, were bright blue and clear
His face had an expression of happiness and cheer
His lips had the form of a great big grin
His hands were clean, his nails neat and trim
His clothes were very clean, his pants had a crease
His shoes just shined that he wore on his feet
He was a very busy man, day after day
Doing his work as time slipped fast away
He laughed and joked with his neighbors and friends
As a garden tool or a mower he'd lend
Food for his stomach and food for his soul
Were both supplied as this man met his goals
This man's life is unbelievable but true
Will the life of this man reflect in you?

People

Some people are smart

Some are stupid

Some are old

Some are young

Some are fat

Some are slim

Some will frown

Some will grin

Some are tall

Some are short

Some are happy

Some are sad

Some are mammas

Some are dads

People, people

In their own way

Help run the world

For another day

Quiet Time

It's just the right time of day for a man
Who likes to sit and daydream
Billions of waves on the river have calmed
And the water flows lazily down stream
Fog o'er the river begins to rise
Fishermen I can faintly see
Frogs on the bank begin to croak
Crickets chirp their tune for me
Trees have all settled down for the night
The rustle among the leaves have gone
Birds go fluttering to and fro
With a beautiful melody of song
Setting among the trees all alone
Only sounds of nature I hear
Which makes me realize even more
That God's presence is very near

Remember

Remember the buckets we had in each hand
As we walked down the road to the well
Oh! How heavy they got before we got home
And the wild fearful tales we would tell

Remember the long john's Mom made us wear
We folded and tucked them just right
As we pulled our long stockings up over the knee
We must have been an awful sight

Remember how we wrestled and rolled in the grass
Sometimes we'd laugh—sometimes we'd cry
Throwed dust from the path in each other's hair
Poured on water—then let it dry

Remember the strawberries we had to pick
The rotten ones we saved in a cup
At the end of the day we mashed the rotten ones
And took turns throwing them at the pup

Remember the hay loft where we used to play
We'd scare the old hens from their nest
We'd swing on a rope out over the hay
The bumblebees were always such pests

Remember the cat so cuddly and warm
Always purring so soft in our ears
But when we pulled her tail and her eyes bugged out
Her screech was something else to hear

Remember? Oh! Yes, I remember
The stories we've so often told
But it seems as tho it were yesterday
Because memories never seem to grow old

Remind Me

God made man from the dust of the earth
And placed him in the Garden of Eden
He was lonely there—God saw his despair
So He took a rib from man and made woman
Remind me.

God knew the task He had for man
He knew man couldn't bear it alone
He made him a mate to help carry the load
Wherever they might wander or roam
Remind me.

She's to make him her hero, her idol, her king
To love him, to honor him and to obey
Never to question the action he takes
Or quarrel with the things he might say
Remind me.

But God also said that man had a duty
To love, protect and take care of his mate
To share with her all the good things of life
As the journey down life's road they make
Remind him.

God said, "The two of you shall be as one."
To serve God the best that you can
To help save souls for God's kingdom above
This is the task for woman and man
Remind us.

That Old Apple Tree

A crooked old apple tree sits high on a hill
Her tiny round apples are as yellow as gold
She bends and sways with the wind and rain
And the bark on her trunk says she's growing quite old

Many a story has been told about the old apple tree
And the rock ledge that lays beneath her roots
Many lovers have quarreled, many lovers made plans
As they sit on the ledge or trod leaves underfoot

As the lovers held hands 'neath the old apple tree
A lovers hut she made, dipping her branches to the ground
Then she listened in silence, had patience galore
As she sometimes smiled, sometimes frowned

Many secrets the old apple tree holds in her heart
They're secrets that will never be told
As she bends and sways with the wind and rain
Then stands there in silence and grows old

Thoughts

Oh! The thoughts a Mother ponders
When in her womb she first conceives
She puts her faith and trust in Jesus
For in Him she doth believe
Oh! The love that is so lavish
Upon this innate she doth bestow
For it is the life she liveth
That will help this wee one grow
Oh! The prayers she offers daily
From the morning until night
As this wee one blossoms in her bosom
And flourishes with strength and might
Oh! The wonders of that moment
When first they lay it in her arms
As she comforts and consoles it
To protect it from all harm
Oh! The miracle of Jesus
As He giveth life in birth
From a Mother and a Father
He created from particles of earth

Thoughts

Smile and the world smiles with me
Cry and I cry alone
Can you help?
Probably not
You haven't walked where I walked
You haven't done the things I've done
My fears were not your fears
You haven't loved like I have loved
Can you help?
No way!
Smile and the world smiles with me
But cry and I cry alone

Time

Time—what is time?

I can't see it—I can't feel it
I can't make it—I can't mold it
I can't take it—I can't give it
I can't control it—I can't save it

Just four little letters that make a word
A word you so often have heard
The meaning is as powerful as it can be
Just four little letters that spell TIME

God gives it to us freely
God takes it quickly away
There is just no way of knowing
How long it might stay

We must use it very wisely
While it's ours to use
We must not use it foolishly
It's not ours to abuse

I can't see it—I can't feel it
I can't make it—I can't mold it
I can't take it—I can't give it
I can't control it—I can't save it

TIME—what is time?

Water

We've read all about it since days of old
They called it water so the stories go
Then as time passed and history unfolds
We became educated—now we call it H_2O
It doesn't matter what it's called—it's only a name
You'll find the components are still the same
This water was made for mankind to use
It wasn't made for us to abuse
We're educated-we know just what to do
To have safe drinking water for me and you
So into our water ways we dump garbage and trash
We haven't learned a thing from out of the past
Then we use harsh chemicals to make it pure
Our bodies work hard to absorb it—that's for sure
Put poison in our system to make us happy and healthy?
No way—we're only making somebody else wealthy!

What Have I Done With My Life

Now as daylight fades and darkness falls
And the years pass swiftly away
I pause for a moment and I ask myself
What have I done with my life today?

Have I visited an elderly neighbor
Who sat in a room all alone
Did I take a flower or speak or smile
Or hold their hand in my own

Did I ask a teenager if I might help
With the problems that trouble their mind
Or help with their homework after school
Or maybe just listen and chat, to pass time

Have I played volleyball or maybe dress-up
With a grandson or granddaughter today
Did we whisper, giggle, and share our secrets
That children do in their own special way

Did I smile or pause or stop and visit
With a cripple or mental patient I might see
Did I stop and lift up my eyes to God
And say "Please, God have mercy on these."

Now as daylight fades and darkness falls
And the years pass swiftly away
I pause for a moment and I ask my self
What have I done with my life today?

W-H-Y

Why were stars put out in space
Why are they always running a race
Why are clouds fluffy and white
Why don't they hide and get out of sight
Why does the wind cut like a knife
Why does thunder roar and lightning strike
Why does the sun shine down from the sky
Why do birds learn how to fly
Why do roses smell so good
Why do we cut trees for wood
Why is the snow so crunchy and white
Why are raindrops so wet and so light
Why do rabbits hide in the ground
Why do snakes crawl all around
Why are the meadows so flat and green
Why is water so clear in a stream
Why are hills so high and steep
Why are valleys so long and deep
Questions—questions but no revelation
The answers are God's. He made this creation.

CATEGORY

15

WHIMSICAL

Burp

A burp's a burp
If it's done just right
But a burp's a belch
In the middle of the night

Burp—Slurp

A burps to slurp, a belch to squelch
It's all over, it was easy
But in the middle of the night, without a light
It was messy, it was greasy.

Sleepy Town

Lay your little ole toggin down
And close your little ole eyes
Go atoo the sleepy town
And float up to the skies
To the land of milk and honey
Where the sugar plums grow
Candy canes and lollipops
All standin' in a row
Little ole teddy bears
With fuzzy fur
Little ole kitty cats
That just purr and purr
Fuzzy little lambs
That just never, never cry
Little ole puppy dogs
That just sit and sigh
Now that's where (child's name) wants to go
To the land of milk and honey
Where the sugar plums grow

Sleepy-Time

As I scamper into my jammies
And snuggle down in bed
Pull the covers way up high
And cover up my head
I like to dream a dream or two
Just doze and snore a mite
Then listen-listen to the rain
As it softly falls tonight

Tear Drop

Tis only a tear drop
I thought to myself
As it fell on my cheek
Then another I felt
Another and another
And then I knew
It couldn't be a tear drop
It must be the dew
But another, still another
And as I looked toward the sky
My face was so wet I thought I had cried
But it's raining, so softly
Not tear drops at all
But it seemed so at first
When they began to fall

Then and Now

They met—spoke—sighed
Fell in love—laughed—cried
He wooed her at her papa's home
They were seldom ever alone
He knew if he ever got to kiss
This maiden of heavenly bliss
She would have to be his wife
And live together all their life
That was love in mamma's day
Now it's done a different way
He whistles at her walk and wiggle
They stop—kiss—giggle
Dig this date, man alive
Just two beatniks full of jive
The stage today for a modern date
Is a hotrod car like a Ford V8
Main street is where they drag and race
And talk of atom bombs and space
They go steady—a week—then marry
Time passes fast—no time to tarry
This is love in daughter's day
This is how it's done the modern way

Goodbye

God put us on earth and gave us free will
To choose our own path day by day
None of us know for sure what we will find
When we get to the end of life's way
But one thing I know, I made my choice
About where I wanted to send my soul
I decided years ago, to live my life for Jesus
And set Heaven as my goal
I've tried with the help of Almighty God
To raise my family the best that I could
I know many times I have stumbled and fell
Many things I haven't done that I should
But I've taught you about God, you've all been baptized
You know what God wants you to do
I've guided and prayed for you all of these years
Now the rest I must leave up to you
So now that I'm leaving, I'll ask just once more
Please don't live your life here in vain
Live everyday as if it were your last
For you won't live that day again
My eyelids are heavy—come kneel by my bed
Hold my hand—now please don't weep
Say a little prayer to Jesus for me
While I slowly drift off to sleep.